SATURN

MURRAY "OAK" TAPETA

Norwood House Press

Cataloging-in-Publication Data

Names: Tapeta, Murray.
Title: Saturn / Murray Tapeta.
Description: Buffalo, NY : Norwood House Press, 2026. | Series: Outer space | Includes glossary and index.
Identifiers: ISBN 9781978574892 (pbk.) | ISBN 9781978574908 (library bound) | ISBN 9781978574915 (ebook)
Subjects: LCSH: Saturn (Planet)--Juvenile literature.
Classification: LCC QB671.T374 2026 | DDC 523.46--dc23

Published in 2026 by
Norwood House Press
2544 Clinton Street
Buffalo, NY 14224

Copyright © 2026 Norwood House Press
Designer: Rhea Magaro
Editor: Kim Thompson

Photo credits: Cover, p. 1 Elena11; p. 5, 9-14, 21 NASA; p. 6, 15 Artsiom P/Shutterstock.com; p. 7 yurakrasil/Shutterstock.com; p. 8 Synthetic Messiah/Shutterstock.com; p. 16 Billion Photos/Shutterstock.com; p. 17 van van/Shutterstock.com; p. 18 Merlin74/Shutterstock.com;

All rights reserved. No part of this book may be reproduced in any form without permission in writing from the publisher, except by a reviewer.

Printed in the United States of America

Some of the images in this book illustrate individuals who are models. The depictions do not imply actual situations or events.

CPSIA compliance information: Batch #CSNHP26: For further information contact Norwood House Press at 1-800-237-9932.

TABLE OF CONTENTS

Where Is Saturn?..4

How Was Saturn Discovered? 8

What Is It Like on Saturn?....................................10

Has Saturn Been Explored?..................................19

Glossary 22

Thinking Questions..23

Index 24

About the Author 24

Where Is Saturn?

Our **solar system** has eight planets. Saturn is the sixth planet from the Sun. It is almost ten times wider than Earth. It is the second largest planet after Jupiter.

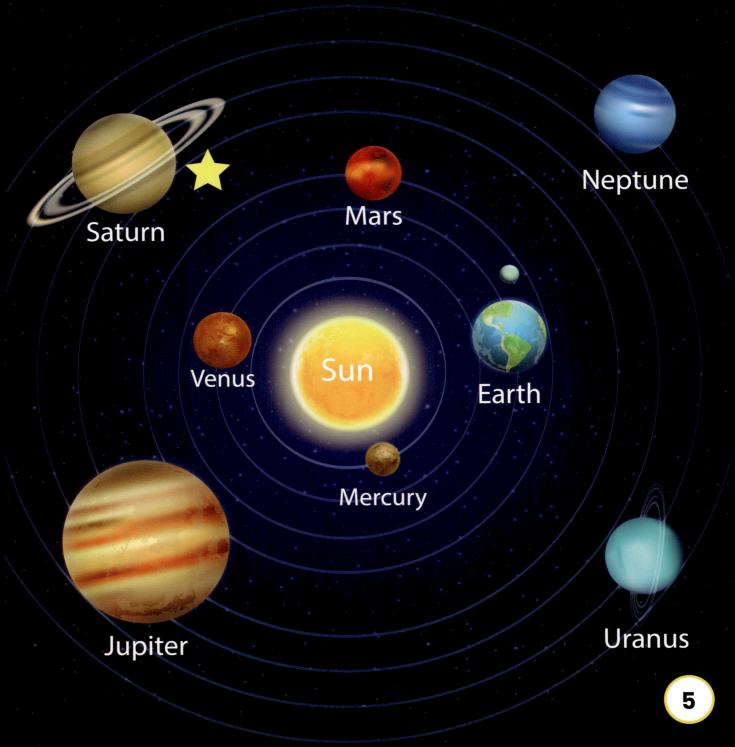

Saturn is about 890 million miles (almost 1.5 billion kilometers) from the Sun. Getting from Earth to Saturn would take around two years.

One year on Saturn lasts about 10,756 Earth days. That is more than 29 Earth years. It takes Saturn that long to **orbit** the Sun.

How Was Saturn Discovered?

Ancient people noticed Saturn in the night sky. It looked like a bright yellow and white star. They named the planet Saturn after the Roman god of farming.

Italian **astronomer** Galileo Galilei first saw Saturn through a **telescope** in 1610.

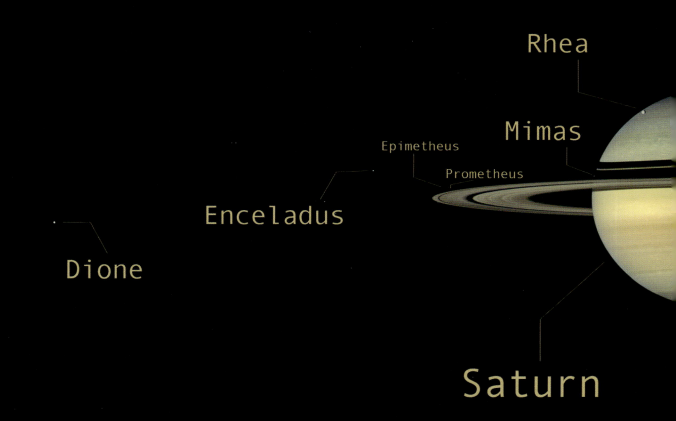

What Is It Like on Saturn?

You could not stand on Saturn. It does not have a solid surface. The planet is mostly made of the gases **hydrogen** and **helium**.

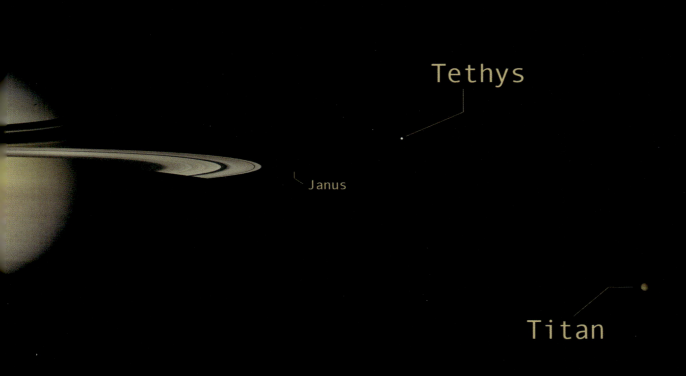

There are 146 moons in Saturn's orbit. That is more than any other planet in our solar system!

Saturn is famous for its beautiful rings. It is called "the ringed planet." Scientists think two icy moons crashed into each other long ago. Saturn's rings are made of the shattered pieces of those moons.

Saturn has a thick **atmosphere**. The weather is windy and stormy. Sometimes, white spots appear on the planet. They are giant storms.

Saturn is freezing cold. The living things we know could not survive there.

Gravity on Saturn is a little stronger than on Earth. A person who weighs 100 pounds (45 kilograms) on Earth would weigh 107 pounds (49 kilograms) on Saturn.

Scientists think Saturn formed nearly five billion years ago. Gravity pulled together swirling dust and gas. Over time, the giant planet formed.

Has Saturn Been Explored?

Saturn is made of gas, so nothing can land there. Scientists have sent four **satellites** to fly close to the planet. They have sent photos and data back to Earth.

In 2028, the spacecraft *Dragonfly* will fly to Saturn's icy moon Titan. It will land in 2034. *Dragonfly* will look like a giant drone. It will look for signs of life.

Glossary

astronomer (uh-STRAH-nuh-mer): a scientist who studies objects in the sky, including planets, galaxies, and stars

atmosphere (AT-muhs-feer): the mixture of gases that surrounds a planet; air

gravity (GRAV-i-tee): an invisible force that pulls objects toward each other and keeps them from floating away

helium (HEE-lee-uhm): a light, colorless gas that does not burn

hydrogen (HYE-druh-juhn): a gas with no smell or color that is lighter than air and that easily catches fire

orbit (OR-bit): to follow a curved path around a larger body in space

satellites (SAT-uh-lites): spacecrafts sent into orbit around a planet, moon, or other object in space

solar system (SOH-lur SIS-tuhm): the Sun and everything that orbits around it

telescope (TEL-uh-skope): an instrument that helps people see distant objects

Thinking Questions

1. Where did the planet Saturn get its name?

2. Describe the weather on Saturn.

3. What is Saturn famous for?

4. How did Saturn's rings form?

5. How many moons does Saturn have?

Index

Dragonfly 20

Earth 4, 6, 7, 16, 19

Galilei, Galileo 9

gravity 16, 17

moons 10, 11, 13, 20

orbit 7, 11

rings 13

Sun 4, 6, 7

Titan 11, 20

weather 14, 15

About the Author

Murray "Oak" Tapeta was born in a cabin without plumbing in Montana. Growing up in the great outdoors, he became a lover of nature. He earned the nickname "Oak" after climbing to the top of an oak tree at the age of three. Oak loves to read and write. He has written many books about events in history and other subjects that fascinate him. He prefers spending time in the wilderness with his dog Birchy.